FUELING THE FUTURE

Fossil Fuels and Biofuels

Elizabeth Raum

Heinemann Library
Chicago, Illinois

Photo research by Rebecca Sodergren and Hannah Taylor
Illustrations by Jeff Edwards
Designed by Richard Parker and Q2A Solutions
Originated by Chroma Graphics (Overseas) Pte Ltd
Printed and bound in China by Leo Paper Group

12 11 10 09 08
10 9 8 7 6 5 4 3 2 1

Library of Congress Cataloging-in-Publication Data
Raum, Elizabeth.
 Fossil fuels and biofuels / Elizabeth Raum.
   p. cm. -- (Fueling the future)
 Includes bibliographical references and index.
 ISBN-13: 978-1-4329-1562-9 (hc)
 ISBN-13: 978-1-4329-1568-1 (pb)
 1. Biomass energy--Juvenile literature. 2. Fossil fuels--Juvenile literature. I. Title.
 HD9502.5.B542R38 2008
 333.95'39--dc22
                            2007050861

Acknowledgments
The author and publisher are grateful to the following for permission to reproduce copyright material:
©Alamy pp. 6 (Phillip Scalla), 24 (Arctic Images); ©Corbis pp. 16 (Hulton-Deutsch Collection), 9, 12 Corbis
Royalty Free; ©FLPA p. 25 (Holt/Angela Hampton); ©Getty Images pp. 4 (Taxi), 14, 23 (Visuals Unlimited),
18 (Iconica/Peter Cade), 20 (The Image Bank); ©NASA p. 21; ©Reuters p. 22 (Claudia Daut); ©Rex Features
p. 17 (Eye Ubiquitous); ©Science Photo Library p. 5 (Roger Harris); ©Still Pictures pp. 10 (Ullstein-Klein), 15,
26 (Joerg Boethling), 19 (Mark Edwards), 27 ©Photolibrary/Uppercut Images.

Cover photograph of a field of corn in summer reproduced with permission of ©Getty Images/Taxi. Cover
background image of blue virtual whirl reproduced with permission of ©istockphoto.com/Andreas Guskos.

The publishers would like to thank David Hood of the Centre for Alternative Technology for his assistance in
the preparation of this book.

Every effort has been made to contact copyright holders of any material reproduced in this book. Any
omissions will be rectified in subsequent printings if notice is given to the publishers.

Disclaimer
All the Internet addresses (URLs) given in this book were valid at the time of going to press. However, due
to the dynamic nature of the Internet, some addresses may have changed, or sites may have changed or
ceased to exist since publication. While the author and publishers regret any inconvenience this may cause
readers, no responsibility for any such changes can be accepted by either the author or the publishers.

Contents

Some words are shown in bold, **like this**. You can find out what they mean by looking in the glossary.

Most of the Earth's **energy** comes from the sun. Sunlight warms and lights the Earth every day. The sun's rays contain energy that is **absorbed** (taken in) by plants and animals. The plants and animals use what they need each day to work, move, and grow. They store the rest.

Wood gives off energy from the sun when it is burned.

Stored energy is called **potential energy**. Early people learned to use the potential energy stored in plants. When they burned wood to produce heat and light they were using the potential energy stored in trees. Wood was one of the earliest **fuels** used on Earth. Today we call fuels that come from plants **biofuels**.

Some people still use wood to heat their homes and cook their food. More often, however, we use **fossil fuels**. Fossil fuels include coal, natural gas, and petroleum (oil).

The remains of ancient plants and animals turned into fossil fuels over millions of years.

What are fossil fuels?

Fossil fuels contain energy that was stored in ancient plants and animals. After the plants and animals died, their remains were buried under layers of mud. As the earth shifted, the rotting plant and animal **matter** was pressed into layers of mud and heated. Shifting earth drove the matter deeper and deeper beneath layers of rock. Gradually, the plant and animal matter broke down to form coal, natural gas, and petroleum.

Fuel from dinosaur bones

Dinosaurs began roaming the Earth about 230 million years ago. Dinosaurs and other ancient plants and animals are the source of the fossil fuels we use today. Of course, not all ancient plants and animals became fuel. Many were preserved as fossils and are buried near the Earth's surface. Others can be seen in museums around the world.

Before they can be used, **fossil fuels** must be recovered from underground or underwater and brought to the surface. They are then sent to **refineries** where they are turned into usable **fuel**. Often they must be transported great distances from where they are found to where they are needed. Coal, natural gas, and petroleum are different forms of fossil fuels.

Some coal is located near the Earth's surface, but in other places, miners go deep underground to dig it out.

What is coal?

Coal is a kind of rock found in almost every country in the world. When coal is burned, it releases **energy** in the form of heat. **Power plants** use the heat to produce electricity. Some people heat their homes with coal.

Mining coal is dangerous work because mines can collapse. Breathing coal dust damages the lungs.

Coal is not renewable. **Renewable** energy can be replaced over time. Scientists believe that there is enough coal to last about 155 years. When it is gone, there is no more.

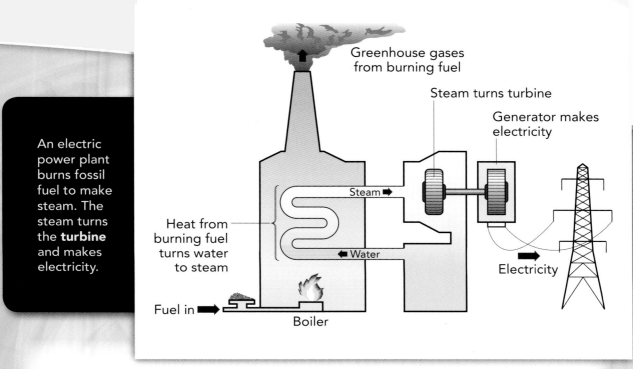

An electric power plant burns fossil fuel to make steam. The steam turns the **turbine** and makes electricity.

Greenhouse gases from burning fuel

Steam turns turbine

Generator makes electricity

Heat from burning fuel turns water to steam

Steam ➡

◀ Water

Electricity ➡

Fuel in ➡

Boiler

What is natural gas?

Natural gas is a colorless, odorless gas composed mostly of **methane**. Natural gas is pumped from underground wells to the Earth's surface. Pipelines carry it to where it is needed. When burned, natural gas gives off energy that is used for heating, cooking, and generating electricity. It is used in homes, schools, and factories.

Like coal, natural gas is not renewable. Experts predict that there is enough natural gas in the world to last at least 120 to 175 years.

Fossil fuel facts

In 2005, 81 percent of the energy used worldwide came from fossil fuels. Oil was the most used fuel (35 percent), followed by coal (25.3 percent) and natural gas (20.7 percent).

What is petroleum?

Petroleum, or oil, is a thick liquid found underground or under the ocean. Like coal and natural gas, petroleum is a fossil fuel formed millions of years ago from decayed plants and animals. Huge drilling **rigs** bring the oil to the surface where it is stored in tanks. Then it goes to a refinery where it is turned into usable fuel. Gasoline, diesel fuel, and home heating oil are all made from petroleum.

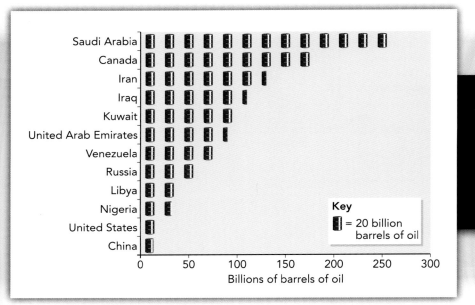

Billions of barrels of oil

Key

= 20 billion barrels of oil

This chart shows which countries have the largest reserves of oil.

Are there problems with oil?

Like coal and natural gas, oil is not renewable. Scientists think that the world will run out of oil in 40 to 60 years. Oil is only found in some regions, so it must be shipped around the world.

Sometimes oil spills from tanker ships and leaks into the ocean. Most spills are caused by accidents when oil tankers are being loaded or unloaded. The biggest spills happen when boats run into rocks, icebergs, or other ships. Not only is the oil wasted, but the spilled oil **pollutes** (dirties) the ocean and kills birds and sea animals.

Oil kills millions of birds every year. Even a tiny glob of oil no bigger than a penny can kill a bird. When a bird tries to spread an oil-covered wing, the feathers stick together and the bird cannot fly or protect itself from the cold. Birds also die from swallowing oil.

Petroleum is used in making plastic toys.

The many uses of petroleum

Petroleum is used for many things. For example, chemicals in petroleum are used to preserve food (keep it fresh) and to make medicines. The rubber used in running shoes comes from petroleum. Many fabrics, including those in curtains, carpets, and wrinkle-free clothing, come from petroleum. Plastics contain petroleum products. The wax in milk cartons, shoe polish, and some candles comes from petroleum.

Why Do We Need Alternative Fuels?

Fossil fuels provide reliable **energy** for electricity, transportation, and home heating, but they are not **renewable**. At some point in the future, we will run out of fossil fuels.

There are also other problems with fossil fuels. One problem is that they cause **pollution**. Waste gases given off by cars, factories, and coal-burning **power plants** are especially dangerous for children, older adults, and people with heart or lung diseases. Oil spills **pollute** the oceans, and mining and drilling operations damage the land.

Power plants that burn coal send pollution, in the form of dirty smoke, into the air.

Fossil fuels also cause **global warming**. When fossil fuels are burned, they send **greenhouse gases** into the air. These gases, which include **carbon dioxide** and **methane**, prevent the sun's heat from leaving the Earth's **atmosphere**. Over the last 100 years, the Earth's temperature has increased by 1 °F (0.6 °C). This doesn't sound like much, but it may be enough to cause major changes in the Earth's climate (general weather pattern). Most scientists agree that our use of fossil fuels is what's causing global warming.

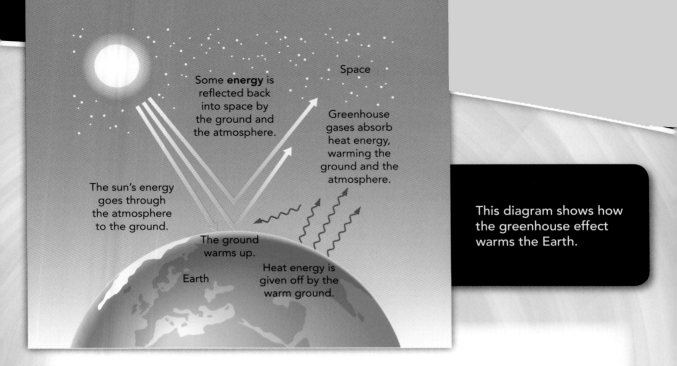

Some **energy** is reflected back into space by the ground and the atmosphere.

Space

Greenhouse gases absorb heat energy, warming the ground and the atmosphere.

The sun's energy goes through the atmosphere to the ground.

The ground warms up.

Earth

Heat energy is given off by the warm ground.

This diagram shows how the greenhouse effect warms the Earth.

Better choices

We need **alternative** fuels that are renewable, easy to find, and available everywhere. We need alternative fuels that do not cause pollution or add to global warming.

The greenhouse effect

In a greenhouse, the glass panels draw in the sun's heat and keep it from escaping. The Earth's atmosphere acts like a greenhouse. The sun's rays enter the atmosphere, and greenhouse gases produced by plants and animals keep the heat from escaping. This is a natural process. Without the **greenhouse effect**, the Earth's average temperature would be 60 °F (33 °C) colder. The natural greenhouse effect keeps the Earth's temperature steady. However, by releasing too many greenhouse gases into the air, we increase the greenhouse effect, which may cause global warming.

What Is Biomass Energy?

Biomass energy is not new. "Biomass" is another word for energy that comes from plant and animal products and remains. For thousands of years, people have used biomass for **fuel**. When we burn wood for heat we are using biomass energy. When we use the oil from plants to make a kind of fuel for trucks and buses, we are using biomass energy. Scientists are studying biomass energy as they look for an **alternative** to **fossil fuels**.

When any kind of biomass is used as fuel, it is often called **biofuel**. Wood is a familiar source of biomass energy. When biomass is used to provide electric power, it is often called **biopower**. Many kinds of trees and grasses can be burned in **power plants** to provide electricity.

Trees are a source of biomass energy.

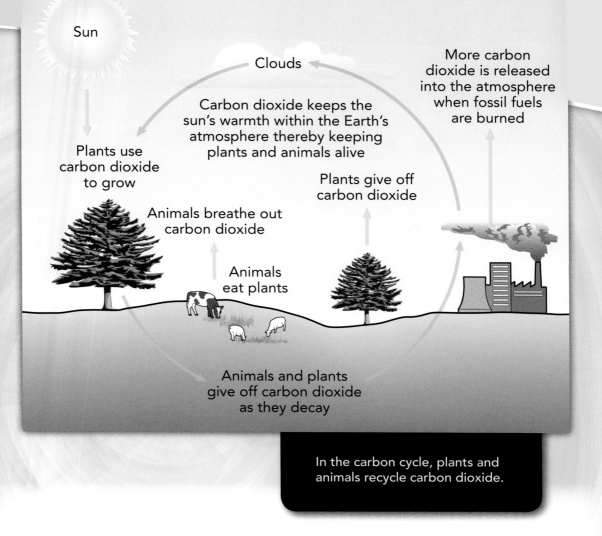

Sun

Clouds

Carbon dioxide keeps the sun's warmth within the Earth's atmosphere thereby keeping plants and animals alive

More carbon dioxide is released into the atmosphere when fossil fuels are burned

Plants use carbon dioxide to grow

Plants give off carbon dioxide

Animals breathe out carbon dioxide

Animals eat plants

Animals and plants give off carbon dioxide as they decay

In the carbon cycle, plants and animals recycle carbon dioxide.

The carbon cycle

All living things contain **carbon**. For life to continue, carbon must be recycled (used again and again). This is called the **carbon cycle**.

In the carbon cycle, plants take in **carbon dioxide**. This is a gas in the air that contains carbon. Plants use carbon dioxide to help them grow. Then animals eat the plants and use the carbon to help them grow. When animals breathe, they give off carbon dioxide, which can be recycled by plants. When plants and animals die, carbon in them is released into the soil and air. It can then be used all over again by growing plants and animals. Carbon dioxide released by fossil fuels overloads the carbon cycle, which leads to **global warming**.

Energy plants

Today scientists and farmers are working together to find which plants work best as biofuels. Some trees and grasses are ideal **energy crops**. Good energy crops are those that are not needed for food and grow back quickly.

Switchgrass is an energy crop.

Switchgrass

Switchgrass once fed the buffalo that roamed the Great Plains of the United States. Switchgrass grows to a height of 6 feet (1.8 meters). Today many farmers grow switchgrass to feed cattle or as a ground cover on land that is not usable for growing crops. Plant scientists say that switchgrass is an excellent energy crop. Scientists in Canada have made small solid pieces out of switchgrass. These can be burned in stoves to heat homes. Switchgrass can be burned to provide energy to electrical power plants. It can also be made into a fuel called **ethanol** and used in cars instead of gasoline.

Jatropha

For many years, farmers in the African country of Mali thought of the jatropha plant as a bothersome weed. Recently scientists discovered that jatropha is a good energy plant. Jatropha seeds produce oil that can run electrical **generators** or cars. Many people in countries like Mali live far from electric power lines. Jatropha may provide the energy they need for lighting, cooking, and running small machines. Private companies are working with local farmers in Mali, as well as in Swaziland, China, India, and the Philippines, to produce biofuel from jatropha seeds.

Like switchgrass, jatropha is called an energy crop because it cannot be used as food. It grows in rocky fields where food crops cannot grow. However, some experts worry that poor farmers may be driven off their land when energy companies purchase the land to grow jatropha or other energy crops.

The seeds of the jatropha plant are used as a biofuel.

Ethanol

Ethanol is a biofuel that can be used to replace gasoline. Many of the first cars ran on ethanol because it was cheap and easily available. In the 1920s, gasoline costs decreased, so drivers switched from ethanol to gasoline. However, as gas prices began rising in the 1980s, some people returned to using ethanol.

Corn, sugar beets, and sugarcane are often used to make ethanol. To make ethanol from corn, the kernels are ground up, mixed with water, and heated. Natural chemicals break the corn down into sugars. Adding **yeast** turns the sugars into ethanol. Most ethanol today is made in **refineries** near farming areas and shipped by truck to gas stations.

Some early cars, like this Model T, used ethanol.

What is biodiesel?

Biodiesel fuel can be used to replace diesel fuel, a petroleum product. Biodiesel can be made from natural plant oils, like soybeans and jatropha, or animal fats. New trucks and buses can use pure biodiesel fuel. Most vehicles, however, can use a combination of 20 percent biodiesel fuel and 80 percent normal diesel. Pure biodiesel might break down engine parts in some older vehicles.

This farmer is bringing sugarcane to a refinery where it will be made into ethanol.

In the United States, only about 1,200 gas stations sell ethanol. However, in Brazil, it is widely available and most cars run on ethanol made from sugarcane. Brazil is the world's largest user of ethanol and biodiesel fuels.

Flexible fuel vehicles

Flexible fuel vehicles (FFVs) are made especially to run on either gasoline or a mixture of 85 percent ethanol and 15 percent gasoline, called E85. Carmakers started producing FFVs in the 1980s. In Brazil, 85 percent of all cars sold are FFVs. There are more than six million FFVs on the roads in the United States today. This includes cars, vans, and pickup trucks.

Plant waste is another form of **biofuel**. Plant waste includes materials such as branches left over from logging and sawdust left over from construction projects. In cities, people often throw out cardboard packaging and yard waste.

These materials can be burned for heating, cooking, or making electricity. A new way of using this **energy** is called **co-firing**. In co-firing, **biomass** is burned with coal. A mix of 20 percent biomass and 80 percent coal reduces the **greenhouse gases** sent into the **atmosphere** while still providing reliable energy.

Cow manure is a good source of energy.

This machine, called a biogas digester, turns manure into biofuel.

Cow energy

Animal waste is also a source of biomass energy. Cow manure contains **methane** gas, which can be used to make electricity. Cow manure is collected and put into a biogas digester sunk into the ground. The tank heats the manure, releasing methane gas. Methane gas leaves the tank through a pipe and goes directly into homes and businesses. Extra methane can be pumped into the power company pipelines. Several farms in the United States use this system to provide their own electricity. They sell the leftover power to the local power companies.

In Tanzania and other African countries, farmers are using methane gas from cow manure for lighting and cooking. Many people in rural Africa do not have electricity, so using animal waste is a good choice. People in India are also making good use of methane for energy.

Africa's energy choice

Biomass energy is the most common form of energy used in Africa. In the Congo, Ethiopia, and Tanzania, over 90 percent of the energy used is biomass energy. Most of that energy comes from wood. Biomass energy accounts for only 2.3 percent of energy use in the United States. It accounts for less than 1 percent of energy use in the United Kingdom.

Many cities and towns dispose of waste materials in a landfill like this one. Using this garbage to make energy makes sense.

Fuel from garbage

More than half of the materials in a typical **landfill** (garbage dump) are biomass. As they decay, they give off methane gas. Several plants throughout the world are designed to capture methane gas and use it to produce electricity. One household waste treatment plant in the Canary Islands, off the coast of Africa, turns up to 75,000 tons of waste a year into gas that provides electricity to several small villages. Sewage treatment plants are working on similar programs to turn human waste into gas.

In Uganda, waste from sawdust, wood chips, the hulls (outer coverings) of coffee beans, and paper is mixed with water and pressed into little lumps. These can be burned to heat homes.

Are Biofuels Good for the Earth?

There are many advantages to **biofuels**. They are **renewable energy** sources. Plants of one kind or another grow everywhere. Farmers and scientists are finding new uses for plants every day. Biofuels are not as expensive as **fossil fuels**, and they do not usually need to be transported long distances.

However, selling **energy crops** is a good source of income, so some experts worry that farmers will grow energy crops instead of food crops. Over time, this could cause serious food shortages and add to the problem of world hunger. It is important to find a balance between food crops and energy crops. Some energy crops, like switchgrass and jatropha, grow well on land that is not usable for food crops.

Is using biofuels kinder to the Earth?

Global warming

Experts disagree about whether biofuels will reduce or increase **global warming**. Some claim that using biofuels increases **greenhouse gases**. This is because many crops (especially corn) used as biofuels release twice as much nitrous oxide, a greenhouse gas, as had previously been thought. Other experts disagree. They believe that using biofuels will actually reduce greenhouse gases.

These protestors in Chile want **alternative** fuels that reduce air pollution. Using **biodiesel** fuel rather than diesel would help.

Pollution

Using biomass waste for fuel helps solve the problem of land and water pollution by eliminating piles of rotting garbage. Reducing the use of fossil fuels prevents lung damage caused by burning coal or breathing coal dust.

What's New in Biomass Energy?

Scientists continue to search for new sources of **biomass energy**. Scientists in Japan, Australia, and the United States are now studying tiny algae plants called microalgae. Microalgae have been around for 2.5 billion years. They are one of the Earth's oldest plants. They are also the fastest-growing plants on the Earth. Microalgae grow quickly in both freshwater and saltwater. They take in the sun's energy and store it for later use. If you press microalgae, oil is produced. One scientist suggests that if enough microalgae are grown, they could be used to completely replace petroleum. Microalgae may even be used as jet **fuel**.

Microalgae form a **renewable**, clean energy source. Microalgae can grow on land or water. They grow so quickly that they can be gathered every few days. Many scientists see microalgae as the **biofuel** of the future.

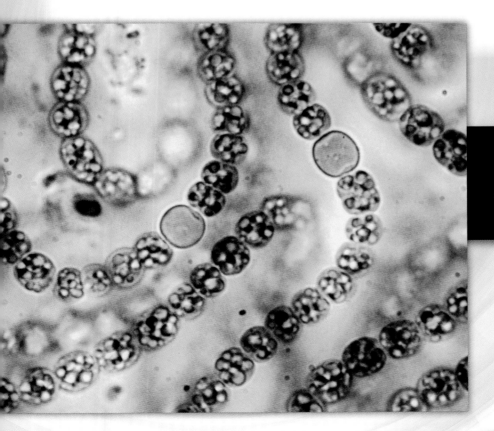

Microalgae double in size every 10 hours.

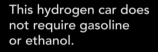
This hydrogen car does not require gasoline or ethanol.

Hydrogen cars

Replacing gas-guzzling cars would help reduce air **pollution** and lessen the problem of **global warming**. Carmakers are developing cars that use **hydrogen fuel cells** instead of gasoline. **Hydrogen** is a clean fuel. It will be a good **alternative** to **fossil fuels** and can be used to power cars, trucks, and **power plants**. A few hydrogen cars are already on the road. More are being designed. The biggest problem now is the lack of hydrogen fuel stations.

Biomass is a source for hydrogen. Scientists plan to use tiny microorganisms to break down plant **matter** into hydrogen. This is a new use for biomass. Perfecting the process will take many years, but scientists look to biomass to help fuel hydrogen cars.

Bioproducts, like this tray made from corn, are biodegradable.

Bioproducts

Bioproducts are products made from biomass. Scientists are developing products made from biomass to replace traditional fossil fuel products. Plant materials can be made into carpet, paint, car parts, cosmetics, household cleaners, soap, and shampoo. Fluids for use in engines, roof coatings, and coatings for the inside of water tanks can be made of biomass. Plastics, glues, and gel for toothpaste are other examples. Bioproducts are **biodegradable**. When we are done with these products, they will break down quickly like all plant matter. We may even use them over again as biofuel.

Petroleum products pollute

A plastic bag made from petroleum does not break down as easily as one made from biomass. It takes about 100 years for a plastic bag made with petroleum to break down in a **landfill**.

World leaders want to reduce the problems of air **pollution** and **global warming** caused by our use of **fossil fuels**. Everyone wants **fuels** that are plentiful, inexpensive, and easy to get. Shipping fossil fuels long distances is costly, and it is not good for the environment.

Biomass energy may be part of the solution. Scientists around the world are studying biomass energy. Business people are setting up **refineries** to harness energy from biomass.

This scientist in India is studying plants for use as biofuels.

Are biofuels the answer?

Biofuels are the kind of **alternative** energy sources that people want. Biofuels are **renewable**. New plants grow every day. Even so, farmers must use care in planting and harvesting energy plants. With care, energy plants are renewable. Inventors will improve the methods and machines used to change biomass waste into usable energy.

Choosing to bike rather than ride in a car is one way to reduce the use of fossil fuels.

What can you do?

Learn about the different kinds of alternative energy. Could you use one instead of fossil fuels? Encourage others to try using less energy, and to switch to new kinds of energy.

Biomass energy is inexpensive, cleaner than fossil fuels, and may reduce land and water pollution. Using it will reduce the damage to the land caused by coal mining and the damage to the ocean and sea creatures caused by oil spills. Scientists disagree about the effect of biomass energy on global warming, but they continue to study the problem.

Growing energy needs

The world's population is expected to reach eight billion by 2030. More people means that we will need more energy, and our energy needs are becoming more complicated. Experts predict that we will use around 60 percent more energy in 2030 than we use today.

In the future, we will be able to choose from several different energy sources. Will you choose fossil fuels or biofuels? Why? This chart may help you decide.

	Fossil Fuel	Notes	Biomass Energy	Notes
Renewable	No	Oil will run out first; coal will last longest	Yes	Careful management will provide constant supply
Readily Available	No	Must be drilled or mined, then transported distances	Yes	Available throughout the world in different forms
Low Cost	No		Yes	May even be free in waste, but processing or refining increases cost
Clean	No	Causes air, land, and water pollution	Yes & no	Reduces land and water damage. Burning biomass causes some air pollution
Reduces Global Warming	No	May be the main cause	?	Scientists disagree and continue to study the question
Other		A few powerful countries control the world's oil supply		Experts fear that land and water needed for growing food may be used for energy crops

Fossil Fuel and Biomass Timeline

2000 BCE	Chinese refine petroleum to light lamps and heat homes.
1750 CE	Pennsylvania is the site of the first oil extracted from a drilled well.
1769	Coal becomes the main **fuel** used by steam-powered trains.
Before the 1890s	Wood is the main fuel for heating, cooking, and making steam used in running factories, trains, and boats.
1890s	Coal replaces wood for making steam; the mass production of automobiles creates a demand for gasoline; electricity begins to replace natural gas for lighting.
1908	Henry Ford's Model T runs on **ethanol**, gasoline, or a combination of the two.
1910s	Coal replaces wood in town and city homes.
1920s	Gasoline becomes the preferred car fuel of choice.
1941–1945	Ethanol production increases due to World War II (petroleum was needed for planes, ships, and other vehicles).
1950	Electricity and natural gas replace wood in homes and factories; oil becomes the most used energy worldwide due to the increase in automobile use.
1960	Iran, Iraq, Kuwait, Saudi Arabia, and Venezuela join to form OPEC (Organization of Petroleum Exporting Countries), an organization to protect their interests as countries that produce oil.
1970s	Oil shortage results when several Arab nations stop selling oil to the United States and the Netherlands.
1984	Ethanol use increases; 163 ethanol plants operate in the United States.
1985	The **biomass** power industry begins to grow in California.
1997	Car manufacturers begin to produce flexible fuel vehicles that can use gas or ethanol.
2000	The first world conference on biomass energy is held in Spain.
2003	Brazil produces the first car to run equally well on either **fossil fuel** or bioethanol.
2007	A U.S. military jet becomes the first aircraft to use **biodiesel** fuel; the U.K. marks the first win in a motorsport race by a truck using biodiesel.

absorb   take in and use

alternative   new or different

atmosphere   layer of gases that surround the Earth

biodegradable   able to break down into natural matter

biodiesel   clean burning fuel made from renewable plant oils such as corn or soybeans

biofuel   plant or animal matter used as fuel

biomass   plant and animal matter

biopower   energy from plant and animal matter

carbon   substance present in all living things

carbon cycle   process by which carbon is recycled in the environment

carbon dioxide   greenhouse gas released when fossil fuels are burned

co-firing   burning biomass fuel with fossil fuel

energy   ability to do work

energy crop   type of plant grown for energy rather than food

ethanol   fuel made from biomass that can be added to petroleum-based fuels, or can replace them altogether

fossil fuel   fuel formed millions of years ago from decayed plants and animals

fuel   something that can be burned to produce heat or power

generator   machine that produces electricity

global warming   increase in temperature of the Earth's land and water

greenhouse effect   rise in temperature on the Earth because certain gases trap energy from the sun

greenhouse gas   type of gas that traps the Earth's heat in the atmosphere. Greenhouse gases include water vapor, carbon dioxide, and methane.

hydrogen   gas that combines chemically with oxygen to form water

hydrogen fuel cell   type of battery that uses hydrogen for energy

landfill   method of solid waste disposal in which waste is buried between layers of dirt so as to fill in low-lying ground

matter   what all things are made of

methane   greenhouse gas formed by decay of biomass

pollute   make dirty or unclean

pollution   something that pollutes (dirties) air, land, or water

potential energy   stored energy that can be used when needed

power plant   factory that makes electricity

refinery   industrial plant that changes raw materials into usable products

renewable   able to be replaced over time

turbine   engine or machine that changes one form of energy to another (often electricity)

rig   machinery used to drill an oil well, and the framework for that machinery

yeast   substance made up of tiny fungi, which is used to turn plant sugar into ethanol

Find Out More

Books

Cheel, Richard. *Global Warming Alert!* New York: Crabtree, 2007.

Graham, Ian. *Fossil Fuels: A Resource Our World Depends On.* Chicago: Heinemann Library, 2005.

Morgan, Sally. *The Pros and Cons of Coal, Gas, and Oil.* New York, Rosen, 2007.

Morris, Neil. *Fossil Fuels.* North Mankato, Minn.: Smart Apple Media, 2006.

Wheeler, Jill. C. *Fossil Fuels.* Edina, Minn.: Checkerboard, 2007.

Websites

Energy Projects and Activities
www1.eere.energy.gov/education/science_projects.html

Energy Kids' Page
www.eia.doe.gov/kids/

Energy Quest Games
www.energyquest.ca.gov/games/index.html

Index